PLANTS AND ANIMALS
OF THE GREAT LAKES

Gareth Stevens
PUBLISHING

BY WALTER LAPLANTE

Please visit our website, www.garethstevens.com. For a free color catalog of all our high-quality books, call toll free 1-800-542-2595 or fax 1-877-542-2596.

Library of Congress Cataloging-in-Publication Data

LaPlante, Walter.
Plants and animals of the Great Lakes / by Walter LaPlante.
p. cm. — (Exploring the Great Lakes)
Includes index.
ISBN 978-1-4824-1203-1 (pbk.)
ISBN 978-1-4824-1193-5 (6-pack)
ISBN 978-1-4824-1438-7 (library binding)
1. Animals — Great Lakes Region (North America) — Juvenile literature. 2. Ecology — Great Lakes Region (North America) — Juvenile literature. I. Title.
QL49.L53 2015
578.0977—d23

First Edition

Published in 2015 by
Gareth Stevens Publishing
111 East 14th Street, Suite 349
New York, NY 10003

Designer: Michael J. Flynn
Editor: Kristen Rajczak

Photo credits: Cover, p. 1 Witold Krasowski/Thinkstock.com; p. 4 D and D Photo Sudbury/ Shutterstock.com; p. 5 http://en.wikipedia.org/wiki/File:Great_lakes_basin.jpg; p. 6 JackK/ Shutterstock.com; p. 7 Jason Patrick Ross/Shutterstock.com; p. 8 Evoken/Shutterstock.com; p. 9 Becky Swora/Shutterstock.com; p. 11 Scott Bauer/AP Images; p. 12 bajinda/ Shutterstock.com; p. 13 Rainer Lesniewski/Shutterstock.com; p. 15 John Kuczala/Stone/ Getty Images; p. 17 Westend61/Getty Images; p. 18 Robert Eastman/Shutterstock.com; p. 19 Lone Wolf Photos/Shutterstock.com; p. 20 Marcia Straub/Shutterstock.com; p. 21 Arto Hakola/Shutterstock.com; p. 22 Daniel Rose/Shutterstock.com; p. 23 hubert/ Shutterstock.com; p. 25 Geoffrey Kuchera/Shutterstock.com; p. 26 William Berry/ Shutterstock.com; p. 27 John McCormick/Shutterstock.com; p. 28 SurangaSL/ Shutterstock.com; p. 29 Bill Frische/Shutterstock.com.

Printed in the United States of America

CPSIA compliance information: Batch #CS15GS: For further information contact Gareth Stevens, New York, New York at 1-800-542-2595.

CONTENTS

Words in the glossary appear in **bold** type
the first time they are used in the text.

LIFE BY THE LAKES

The Great Lakes are five freshwater lakes that form a natural border between Canada and the United States. Lake Huron, Lake Ontario, Lake Michigan, Lake Erie, and Lake Superior are among the 15 biggest lakes in the world! The lakes are part of a vast **ecosystem** that also includes their shorelines and the smaller waterways of the Great Lakes **watershed**.

The plants and animals that live in the Great Lakes region are a major part of the ecosystem. From moose to sugar maple trees, all these organisms have an impact on the health of the Great Lakes **habitats**. Likewise, the region's health also affects the local wildlife.

BIODIVERSITY

"Biodiversity" means the number of different kinds of plants and animals that live in an area. Great biodiversity is a sign of a healthy ecosystem. The more than 35 million people who live around the Great Lakes are part of the lakes' ecosystem. If biodiversity suffers, eventually those people will, too.

This map shows all the US states and Canadian provinces in the Great Lakes watershed. More than 3,500 kinds of plants and animals live in this region.

The high dunes at Sleeping Bear Dunes National Lakeshore in Michigan can give visitors great views across Lake Michigan.

The huge ecosystem of the Great Lakes region includes wetlands, sand dunes, and freshwater habitats of the many fish that live in the lakes and nearby waterways. Hardwood forests of sugar maple, oak, and beech trees grow in the northern Great Lakes region, along with evergreen trees such as spruce and balsam fir.

The sand dunes around the Great Lakes are one of the biggest systems of freshwater sand dunes in the world. Sand dunes are mounds of sand that have been moved by the wind and include many trees and plants, such as the American searocket. They cover thousands of acres of land along the Lake Michigan and Lake Ontario shorelines.

WETLANDS

The Great Lakes watershed has many kinds of wetlands, including marshes, swamps, bogs, and fens. A marsh is a wetland that generally features grasses and reeds, while swamps are wooded wetlands. Bogs have little water flow, acid soil, and many mosses. Fens are similar to bogs, but their soil is less acid. Each type of wetland has its own ecosystem and features, but all provide food and shelter to **migratory** birds such as ducks and geese.

Wetlands provide "nursery" habitats for fish to reproduce and for their offspring to grow.

Some habitats of the Great Lakes region are **unique**. The thousands of acres of freshwater marshes differ greatly around the watershed, from the widespread shoreline wetlands of southwestern Lake Erie to the **delta** marshes of the St. Clair River near Lake Huron.

The alvar lake plains are a habitat found in few other places in the world. This landscape of rock, mostly limestone, has shallow soil and little plant life. A few **rare** plants and animals live there, such as the lakeside daisy. It's only found in a few places in the Great Lakes region, including the Bruce Peninsula in Ontario.

part of the Bruce Peninsula

A SPECIAL PLACE TO LIVE

According to the Environmental Protection Agency (EPA), more than 30 plant **species**, seven kinds of fish, and three types of birds that live in the Great Lakes watershed are "globally rare." A deepwater fish called the cisco is one. The lake sturgeon is another. The dune thistle and Houghton's goldenrod are two plants that only grow in the Great Lakes' sand dunes.

One example of the alvar lake plains in the Great Lakes is found on Kelleys Island in Lake Erie, shown here.

HABITAT HARM

To date, about half of the original wetlands and 60 percent of forests of the Great Lakes watershed have been destroyed. Much of this is due to clearing land to build homes, roads, and businesses. Growing cities mean more people driving cars, which increases air pollution that wildlife in the region breathes in. There's also more trash and human waste that may be disposed of in waterways or poorly constructed landfills. Years ago, industrial waste was dumped in many parts of the Great Lakes region. This has resulted in poor water quality to this day.

When habitats are destroyed or harmed, the animals and plants that live there may die out if they can't find somewhere else to go.

THERE'S HOPE

There are many groups in both the United States and Canada working to protect the habitats and wildlife around the Great Lakes. Their **conservation** efforts include restoring wetlands to their natural state and speaking to those in government about passing laws about water quality. These groups try to focus attention on **endangered** plants and animals of the region, so their populations might increase, too.

Proposed sulfide mining near Lake Superior concerns many conservation groups. Sulfide mining has polluted water and harmed habitats in the past.

Invasive species are another **threat** to the plants and animals of the Great Lakes region. These are plants and animals that have been brought to the area, sometimes accidentally, and reproduce quickly. They take up habitat space and food sources of native species. Some invasive species in the Great Lakes region include the sea lamprey, zebra mussel, and purple loosestrife.

Spiny water fleas are tiny **crustaceans** native to Europe and Asia. They were brought to the Great Lakes in the 1980s by water discharged from ocean ships. Today they're found in all the Great Lakes, where they eat food sources of native fish.

Asian carp

ASIAN CARP

One of the most concerning invasive species is Asian carp. They adapt quickly to new places and have no natural predators in North America. That's one reason their population has grown so quickly since their introduction to the United States in the 1970s. If they enter the Great Lakes, they'll be almost impossible to get rid of.

places Asian carp have been spotted

This map shows where Asian carp have been spotted. They could swim up the Mississippi River and into the canals that connect it to Lake Michigan, but many groups are trying to stop them.

BROOK TROUT

Brook trout live in cool, clear lakes and rivers of the northeastern United States and Canada, including the Great Lakes. They're found as far south as Georgia and throughout the Appalachian Mountains. Some kinds of these fish live in marine areas, too.

Young freshwater brook trout, or fry, eat **aquatic** insects. Adult brook trout eat just about anything they can fit in their mouth! This includes mayflies, frogs, salamanders, and other fish.

City growth and deforestation affect aquatic habitats, often harming brook trout populations. As a result, brook trout conservation projects are ongoing in Ohio, among other Great Lakes states, and Canada.

OVERFISHING

Commercial fishing has long been part of the Great Lakes region's economy. However, too much fishing, or overfishing, has caused some fish populations to fall. Lake sturgeon have had critically low numbers in the Great Lakes region since the early 1900s. The blue pike used to swim in much of Lake Erie, but has been considered extinct since about 1970. Both of these species were greatly overfished.

The brook trout is the state fish of Michigan.

SALMON

Both Atlantic and Pacific salmon are found in the Great Lakes watershed. Atlantic salmon are native to Lake Ontario and the St. Lawrence River, and were introduced to the other Great Lakes around 1972. People began stocking Pacific salmon in the Great Lakes during the 1870s.

Due to overfishing and urban growth, Atlantic salmon completely died out in Lake Ontario by 1900. Both the Canadian government and New York State began to stock Atlantic salmon again in 2012. Part of their efforts include restoring the habitats salmon like. This includes the gravelly stream bottoms in which they nest and lay eggs.

COLD AND DEEP OR WARM AND SHALLOW?

The five Great Lakes are all different from each other as habitats! Lake Superior is the largest Great Lake, and it's cold and deep. Lake Erie, on the other hand, is smaller, warmer, and shallower by comparison. The kinds and numbers of fish that live in each lake differ because of these features. Lake Erie may have as much as 50 percent of the fish living in the lakes!

Salmon that live in the Atlantic Ocean spend part of their life in salt water and part in freshwater. The Atlantic salmon of the Great Lakes live their whole life in freshwater.

CANADA GOOSE

The Canada goose can be found throughout the Great Lakes watershed. Its black head and neck and white cheek patches are familiar to many who live in the region because there are so many of them! In the early 1900s, the Canada goose was in danger of dying out. Conservation efforts have been so successful that some states established Canada goose hunting seasons to keep the population in check.

There are several kinds of Canada goose, and some migrate to the southern United States and Mexico for winter. They live on grassy, marshy land where they can find lots of short grasses to eat.

MIGRATORY BIRDS

The Great Lakes region is the year-round home to many kinds of birds, but millions of birds migrate through the area each spring and fall. The ovenbird winters in Central America and the Caribbean and builds its nest on the floor of Great Lakes hardwood forests during summer. The common loon can also be found building nests and laying eggs near the Great Lakes during the summer.

Some people call flocks of Canada geese pests. One reason is that 50 Canada geese can produce 2.5 tons (2.27 mt) of waste in a year!

BALD EAGLE

The bald eagle is perhaps the most recognizable bird in the United States! A national symbol, these birds are often spotted near water, where they catch fish for food. They can be found in the forests around the Great Lakes, although their range includes much of North America.

Pollution remains a threat to bald eagles. Habitat destruction on shorelines may harm their numbers, too.

Bald eagles were considered a protected species under the Endangered Species Act starting in 1978. It became illegal to hunt them, which helped their populations increase. The banning of DDT, a chemical used in farming, in 1980 benefited bald eagles, too. They were often poisoned by its presence in their habitats. In 2007, the bald eagle was removed from the endangered species list.

BIG BLUE

The great blue heron is the largest kind of heron in North America. It's commonly found in the Great Lakes region during the summer when it builds a nest for its eggs in trees near the lakes, rivers, and wetlands of the area. It migrates south for the winter, but some herons might stay year-round if they can find open water.

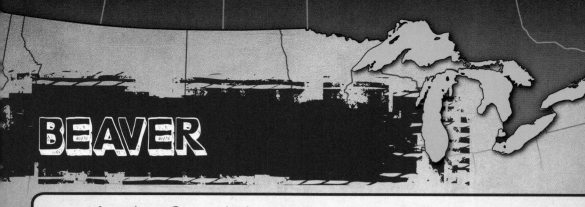

Another Great Lakes animal that nearly died out because of hunting is the American beaver. The beaver's thick fur was prized in trade beginning in the mid-1500s and throughout early North American settlement. Around 1900, beaver populations were dangerously low.

Today, beavers aren't endangered. Trapping continues, especially in parts of Canada, but it's regulated.

Beavers live throughout North America, including in the forests around the Great Lakes. They're known for building dams out of logs, branches, and mud to create the ponds they like to live near. This can cause serious changes to a forest ecosystem, similar to those caused by people!

MAMMALS

The Great Lakes are home to many mammals in addition to beavers. Mammals are warm-blooded animals that have a backbone and hair, breathe air, and feed milk to their young. Little brown bats, moose, river otters, black bears, and coyotes all make their homes in the many habitats in the region.

Beavers can build dams so large they can be seen from space.

GRAY WOLF

Gray wolves can be spotted in the Great Lakes states of Michigan and Minnesota as well as in Ontario. They can live in many kinds of habitats, including forests and grasslands.

Gray wolves are at the top of the Great Lakes region food chain! They like to eat hoofed animals, such as deer and moose, as well as beavers and rabbits. Gray wolves live, hunt, and move in packs of four to seven wolves.

People have long considered gray wolves to be dangerous, though they don't often attack humans. They were commonly killed in the past for hunting pets and farm animals.

MAKING A COMEBACK

The gray wolf used to make its home across North America. These wolves were killed in great numbers and almost died out in the United States by the 1930s. Conservation efforts, including the reintroduction of gray wolves to Yellowstone National Park, helped bring them back! Today, there are about 5,000 living in the lower 48 states. As many as twice that live in Alaska.

The gray wolf population is still only a small percentage of its historic numbers. Conservation groups are fighting to keep the wolves on the national endangered species list until their population rebounds even more.

WHITE PINE

Some of the tallest trees in the state of Michigan are white pines. They may live to be 500 years old! White pines can also be found throughout the Great Lakes region, including in Minnesota, Illinois, Ohio, and the St. Lawrence River valley. They cover about 17 million acres (7 million ha). While that sounds like a lot, it's about half the land the white pine once covered.

White pines are beautiful to look at—but they also have an important role within the Great Lakes ecosystem. Small mammals and birds eat white pine seeds. Bald eagles build their nests in white pines. Black bear cubs climb these trees to hide from predators.

white pine needles

EARTHWORM INVASION!

Scientists are beginning to see signs that earthworms, which are invasive, have changed the soil and forest floor throughout the Great Lakes region, reducing the number of insects. Birds then have less to eat and less plant matter to use to build nests. Even the loss of the smallest living things can harm an ecosystem.

White pine was found to be a valuable, useful wood. Widespread logging contributed to the loss of white pine forests.

SUGAR MAPLE

The sugar maple isn't just a common tree in the Great Lakes region. Its leaf is on the Canadian flag, and it's the state tree of New York!

Sugar maples can grow to more than 100 feet (30.5 m) tall. Their broad, green leaves change to yellow, orange, and red in the fall, and then fall off. The sugar maple gets its name from the maple syrup and sugar it produces. Animals such as squirrels eat the seeds, leaves, and twigs of the sugar maple, too. Its wood is also used for furniture and flooring.

Canadian Flag

CONSERVATION DOLLARS

The natural beauty of the Great Lakes habitats attracts many tourists every year. Bird-watchers, sport fishermen, and hikers visit the dunes, forests, and other areas to see some of the plants and animals included in this book—and thousands more! In order to keep bringing these people in, the wildlife and their habitats need to remain healthy and diverse. It helps the region's economy!

The number of sugar maples is declining due to acid rain changing the soil in parts of the trees' habitat. Acid rain is partly caused by the burning of fuels that produce air pollution.

GLOSSARY

aquatic: having to do with water

conservation: the care of the natural world

crustacean: an animal with a hard shell, jointed limbs, feelers, and no backbone

delta: land shaped like a triangle at the mouth of a river

ecosystem: all the living things in an area

endangered: in danger of dying out

habitat: the natural place where an animal or plant lives

migratory: having to do with migration, or moving to warmer or colder places for a season

rare: uncommon or special

species: a group of plants or animals that are all the same kind

threat: something likely to cause harm

unique: being the only one of its kind

watershed: an area of land whose water drains into a particular river or waterway

BOOKS

Bekkering, Annalise. *Great Lakes.* New York, NY: AV2 by Weigl, 2013.

Greve, Tom. *Freshwater Fish.* Vero Beach, FL: Rourke Publishing, 2012.

WEBSITES

Fish Around the Great Lakes
www.shipwreckexplorers.com/great_lakes_fish.php
Read all about the many fish that live in the Great Lakes, and see what they look like.

Save the Lakes: Kids
www.greatlakeswatershed.org/save-the-lakes-kids.html
Find tips on how to save the Great Lakes and links to other conservation websites.

INDEX